SHORT WALKS
CHEDDAR AND THE MENDIPS

by Rachel Mead

Follow the fingerpost to the summit of Crook Peak (Walk 1)

CONTENTS

Using this guide.. 4
Route summary table 6
Map key 7
Introduction.. 9
  Walking on the Mendip Hills... 9
  When to go... 10
  Where to stay... 11
  Getting around 13

The walks

1.	Crook Peak and King's Wood	15
2.	Dolebury Warren and Rowberrow	23
3.	Beacon Batch and Velvet Bottom	27
4.	Piney Sleights and north of Cheddar Gorge	33
5.	South of Cheddar Gorge	39
6.	Middledown and Bubwith Acres Nature Reserves	43
7.	Cheddar Reservoir and Axbridge	49
8.	Rhynes and droves	55
9.	Ashton Windmill	59
10.	Nyland Hill	63
11.	Westbury-sub-Mendip	69
12.	Ebbor Gorge and Ebbor Wood	73
13.	Priddy and Deer Leap	77
14.	Priddy Nine Barrows and Stockhill Wood	83
15.	Chew Valley Lake and Knowle Hill	89

Useful information 95

USING THIS GUIDE

Routes in this book

In this book you will find a selection of easy or moderate walks suitable for almost everyone, including casual walkers and families with children, or for when you only have a short time to fill. The routes have been carefully chosen to allow you to explore the area and its attractions. Most routes are circular or out-and-back, although some linear walks may be included that use public transport to get back to the start. Although there may be some climbs there is no challenging terrain, but do bear in mind that conditions can sometimes be wet or muddy underfoot. A route summary table is included on page 6 to help you choose the right walk.

Clothing and footwear

You won't need any special equipment to enjoy these walks. The weather in Britain can be changeable, so choose clothing suitable for the season and wear or carry a waterproof jacket. For footwear, comfortable walking boots or trainers with a good grip are best. A small rucksack for drinks, snacks and spare clothing is useful. See www.adventuresmart.uk.

Walk descriptions

At the beginning of each walk you'll find all the information you need:

- start/finish location, with a what3words address to help you find it
- parking and transport information, estimated walking time, total distance and climb
- details of public toilets available along the route and where you can get refreshments
- a summary of the key highlights of the walk and what you might see

Timings given are the time to complete the walk at a reasonable walking pace. Allow extra time for extended stops or if walking with children.

The route is described in clear, easy-to-follow directions, with each waypoint marked on an accompanying map extract. It's a good idea to read the whole of the route instructions before setting out, so that you know what to expect.

Maps, GPX files and what3words

Extracts from the OS® 1:25,000 map accompany each route. GPX files for all the walks in this book are available to download at www.cicerone.co.uk/1254/gpx.

What3words is a free smartphone app which identifies every 3m square of the globe with a unique three-word address, e.g. ///destiny.cafe.sonic. For more information see https://what3words.com/products/what3words-app.

USING THIS GUIDE

Walking with children

Even young children can be surprisingly strong walkers, but every family is different and you may need to adapt the timings given in this book to take that into account. Make sure you go at the pace of the slowest member and choose a walk with an exciting objective in mind, such as a cave, river, waterfall or picnic spot. Many of the walks can be shortened to suit – suggestions are included at the end of the route description.

Dogs

Sheep or cattle may be found grazing on a number of these walks. Keep dogs under control at all times so that they don't scare or disturb livestock or wildlife. Cattle, particularly cows with calves, may very occasionally pose a risk to walkers with dogs. If you ever feel threatened by cattle, you should let go of your dog's lead and let it run free.

Enjoying the countryside responsibly

Enjoy the countryside and treat it with respect to protect our natural environments. Stick to footpaths and take your litter home with you. When driving, slow down on rural roads and park considerately, or better still use public transport. For more details check out www.gov.uk/countryside-code.

The Countryside Code

Respect everyone
- be considerate to those living in, working in and enjoying the countryside
- leave gates and property as you find them
- do not block access to gateways or driveways when parking
- be nice, say hello, share the space
- follow local signs and keep to marked paths unless wider access is available

Protect the environment
- take your litter home – leave no trace of your visit
- do not light fires and only have BBQs where signs say you can
- always keep dogs under control and in sight
- dog poo – bag it and bin it – any public waste bin will do
- care for nature – do not cause damage or disturbance

Enjoy the outdoors
- check your route and local conditions
- plan your adventure – know what to expect and what you can do
- enjoy your visit, have fun, make a memory

ROUTE SUMMARY TABLE

WALK NAME	START POINT	TIME	DISTANCE
1. Crook Peak and King's Wood	White Hart Inn, Cross	3hr	10km (6.2 miles)
2. Dolebury Warren and Rowberrow	The Swan Inn, Rowberrow	2hr	6km (3.7 miles)
3. Beacon Batch and Velvet Bottom	Blagdon	2hr 30min	10km (6.2 miles)
4. Piney Sleights and north of Cheddar Gorge	The Cheddar Cakery, Cheddar	3hr	8.8km (5.5 miles)
5. South of Cheddar Gorge	Edelweiss Cafe, Cheddar	2hr	4.5 km (2.8 miles)
6. Middledown and Bubwith Acres Nature Reserves	Butter Cross, Cheddar	2hr	7.1km (4.4 miles)
7. Cheddar Reservoir and Axbridge	Axbridge	1hr 30min	5km (3.1 miles)
8. Rhynes and droves	Cheddar Reservoir	2hr	9km (5.6 miles)
9. Ashton Windmill	Ashton Windmill, Chapel Allerton	1hr	3.7km (2.3 miles)
10. Nyland Hill	Strawberry Special Inn, Draycott	2hr	5.3km (3.3 miles)
11. Westbury-sub-Mendip	Westbury-sub-Mendip	2hr 30min	5.6km (3.5 miles)
12. Ebbor Gorge and Ebbor Wood	Ebbor Gorge National Nature Reserve	1hr 30min	2.5km (1.6 miles)
13. Priddy and Deer Leap	Priddy Green	2hr	6.5km (4 miles)
14. Priddy Nine Barrows and Stockhill Wood	Stockhill Wood	1hr 30min	5.8km (3.6 miles)
15. Chew Valley Lake and Knowle Hill	Chew Valley Lake	1hr 30min	5km (3.1 miles)

ROUTE SUMMARY TABLE

HIGHLIGHTS
360-degree views and ancient woodland
Iron Age ramparts and wildlife
Highest point on the Mendip Hills
Ancient woodlands and spectacular gorge views
Spectacular gorge views
Two nature reserves and extended views
Historical town, with birdlife and reservoir views
Peaceful watery walk – completely flat!
Windmill and willows – Somerset's rural heritage
Sleepy lanes, farms and one magnificent view
Historic railway walk and nature reserve
Ancient gorge and woodlands
Exceptional views and village life
Bronze Age burial chambers and forest walk
Woodland, lakeside and a hill with a view

SYMBOLS USED ON ROUTE MAPS

(S) Start point

(F) Finish point

(SF) Start and finish at the same place

4 → Waypoint

~ Route line

MAPPING IS SHOWN AT A SCALE OF 1:25,000

DOWNLOAD THE GPX FILES FOR FREE AT
www.cicerone.co.uk/1254/gpx

Goat kids on the cliffs of Cheddar Gorge (Walks 4 and 5)

INTRODUCTION

Soak up incredible views from the top of Crook Peak (Walk 1)

When you step out on one of these walking routes you will be exploring a landscape that was formed millions of years ago. Cheddar Gorge is England's largest gorge and was created naturally by glacial meltwater when a river cut through the landscape. The 5km long gorge is a fascinating natural phenomenon which continues to captivate all who visit.

Cheddar sits in the midst of the Mendip Hills – an area which has been designated as a 'National Landscape'. From the coastal town of Weston-super-Mare in the west to the trendy and vibrant town of Frome in the east, the Mendip Hills stretch up to the Chew Valley in the north of the county and down to Wells, the smallest city in England, in the south. Once you lace up your hiking boots, you'll soon see why the Mendip Hills are adored for their incredibly diverse and spell-binding landscapes.

Walking on the Mendip Hills

The landscape oozes a ruggedness which is loved by walkers as much as by the nimble feral goats who cling to the inland cliffs with surprising ease. Although we are in the Mendip 'Hills', if you aren't so keen on tackling any actual hills, do not worry: some of these walks (for instance Walks 8 and 9) focus on the Somerset Levels, a flatter area of the county where you will be introduced to Somerset's

Exmoor ponies graze the open heath (Walk 3)

traditional farming culture – expect to see withy beds growing willow for basket-making, and orchards bursting with apples for your refreshing glass of Somerset cider.

For walkers seeking a little more of a challenge, then some of the routes in this book do include some elevation. The walk up to Crook Peak (Walk 1), for example, reveals views stretching across to the iconic Glastonbury Tor in one direction, or way over to the Bristol Channel and out to Cardiff in Wales in the other. You may also be keen to 'bag a trig point' at Beacon Batch (Walk 3), the highest point on the Mendip Hills at 325m. The open heathland here is a favourite spot for Somerset's native Exmoor ponies as they graze amongst the heather and gorse, and the area is rich with wildlife.

Please do follow the guidance in this book carefully; although many of these routes follow well-trodden footpaths, some routes take you off the beaten track and as such signage may be limited in some areas.

When to go

Every season will offer walkers a different feel when out on the Mendip Hills. Spring and summer showcase diverse plant life due to the fact that so much of the land has been managed non-invasively. Do keep an eye out for the county flower of Somerset – the Cheddar Pink. At home on the southern-facing limestone grassland slopes, this small, frilly-edged flower is exclusive to Cheddar Gorge, though currently on the Red List of endangered species in Britain. The limestone grasslands are also a favourite with birdlife, including meadow pipits, stonechats and skylarks. Peregrine falcons are known to visit the area and sightings of buzzards and willow warblers are common.

Autumn and winter bring a change in the colour of the leaves and a new lens through which to view the landscape. As the low winter sunshine dapples the carpeted woodland floor, the woodland paths weave through these ancient lands enticing you to explore a landscape with many layers.

Where to stay

Accommodation is available in Cheddar and surrounding villages and towns, to suit all budgets from campsites and B&Bs to cosy rooms in pubs and hotels. Cheddar village itself is the main hub for cafes, restaurants and bars, whereas many of the surrounding villages will have a pub serving locally sourced food, ciders and ales.

Depending on the time of year you may be greeted by high willow rods (Walk 9)

The Cheddar Yeo runs through the village of Cheddar

Getting around

Parts of the Mendip Hills are isolated and public transport is limited, so a car is the easiest way to access many of the walks in this guidebook. With this in mind, all the routes are circular so that you can start and finish where you have parked your car.

There are limited bus options within the Mendip Hills. Details are given for each walk but services are subject to change – check out the latest information at www.firstbus.co.uk. Trains serve Weston-super-Mare (for bus connections to Cheddar) or, if cycling, alight at Yatton to enjoy a ride along the 17km Strawberry Line cycle path to Cheddar, along the track of the old Cheddar Valley railway.

For cyclists National Cycle Network (NCN) route 26 follows the Strawberry Line and terminates in Cheddar (www.strawberryline.org.uk), while routes 3 and 33 connect to the Mendip Hills wider area.

Cheddar Gorge is formed by limestone cliffs (Walk 5)

King's Wood is an ancient woodland

WALK 1
Crook Peak and King's Wood

Start/finish	The White Hart Inn, Cross
Locate	///inclines.swift.ocean
Cafes/pubs	Pub at start
Transport	Bus 48 (limited days)
Parking	Free on-street parking (BS26 2EE)
Toilets	No public toilets on route

Time 3hr
Distance 10km (6.2 miles)
Climb 330m

With spectacular 360-degree views, this walk summits at a distinctive natural landmark

For those of you after a challenging scramble, this walk hits the spot with a mid-walk clamber to the rocky 'summit' of Crook Peak. The terrain underfoot is uneven but the views are worth the additional effort! You'll explore an ancient woodland too.

Crook Peak's rocky outcrop offers panoramic views

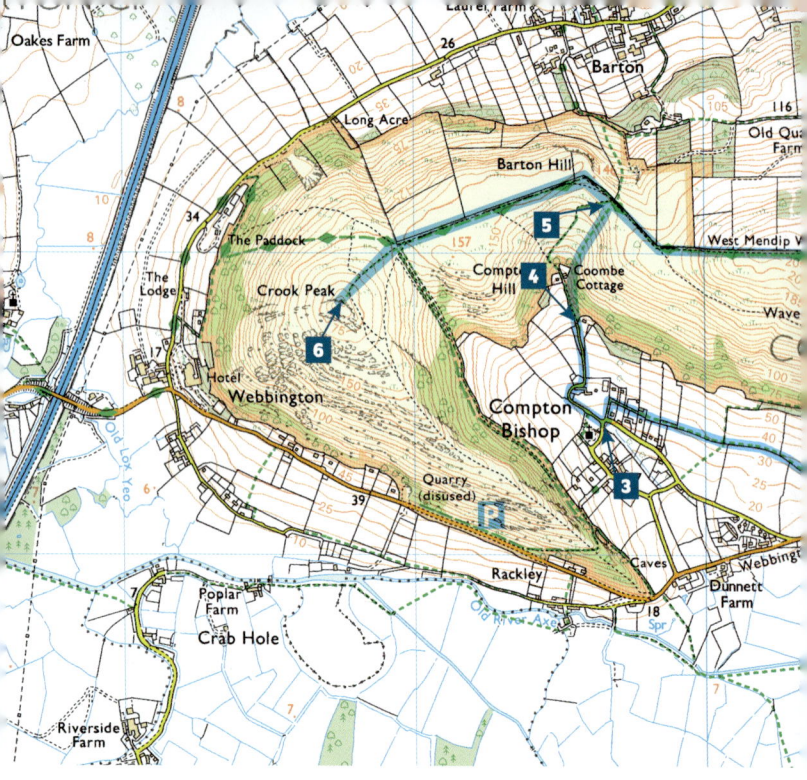

1 With the White Hart pub in **Cross** behind you, pass a cream house with topiary hedging on your right and then Quarry House. Follow the grass verge to the footpath, go through the gate and head uphill. Stone steps to a kissing gate open out to a quarry face. Turn immediately left, keeping the quarry on your right, towards a gate. Go through and bear right to cross the field diagonally. Go through the first kissing gate (ignoring the second one), keep the fence and hedge on your left and walk through a large opening into the next field. Ignore the vehicular gate on the left and head for the footpath gate in the lower left-hand corner of the field, towards **Bourton Farm**.

2 With the farmhouse on your right, follow the footpath down through a kissing gate onto the driveway of the farmhouse and join a lane. Cross the lane to a footpath gate opposite and walk beneath the electricity wires overhead. Keeping the fence to your

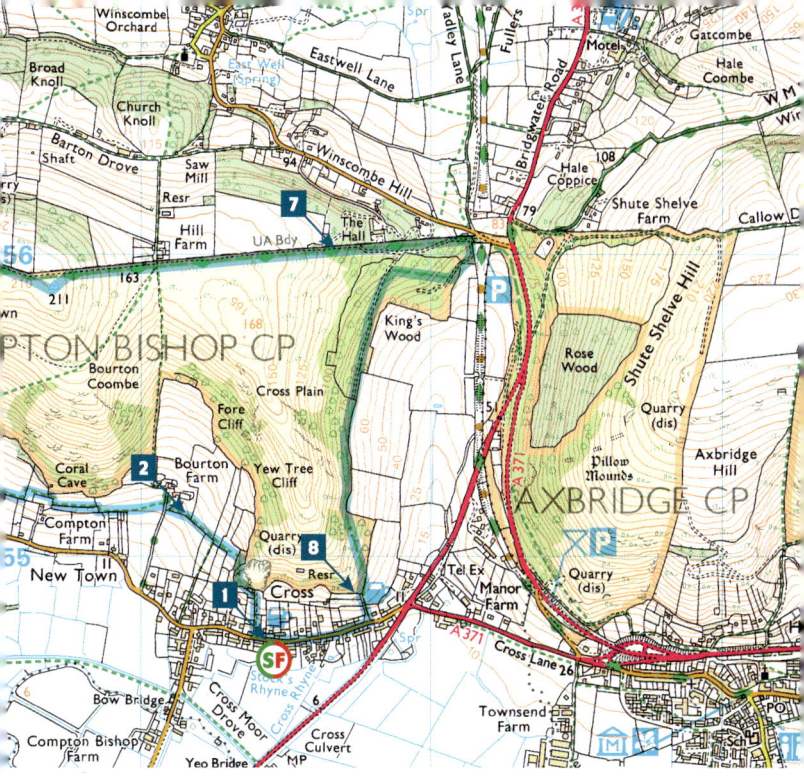

left, pass through a gate, cross the next field and go through another gate. Keep the hedge to your left. Do not use the stile marked 'Private', bypass the farm track on your left and follow the footpath beneath a tree with a water trough to your right. Keep the hedge on your left and follow the path through the fields, beneath an oak tree, through a gate and on through the next field, keeping the hedge on your left. The gate is in the left-hand corner of the field. Keep the hedge on your left – do not divert off this footpath – keep straight on. Go through the footpath gate stating 'Livestock keep gate shut', with stables on your right. Follow ahead. The footpath joins a lane with the church tower seen on your left. The lane curves left and drops down to join Church Lane in **Compton Bishop**.

3 Turn right and immediately right again into Coombe Lane, with the church on your left and Compton

SHORT WALKS CHEDDAR AND THE MENDIPS

House on your right. After about 100m go through a five-bar gate signed 'Private lane Coombe Croft – Coombe Cottage' and take the footpath immediately on your right.

4 The path forks – take the left-hand option with a yellow arrow pointing left (which runs parallel with the lane). The path branches right through the copse and may be obscured by fallen leaves at certain times of year but a natural path will lead you up (ignore any paths which lead left or downhill). The gradient gets steeper, then a single wooden post with a yellow arrow greets you at the top.

5 Follow the arrow towards fingerposts by the drystone wall. Do not pass through the gateway but follow signs left to **Crook Peak**, keeping the drystone wall on your right. The climb up is gradual before a rocky scramble at the summit – you will need to use hands as well as feet to get to the top with its panoramic views. The name Crook Peak may be linked to old English word 'cruc' meaning 'pointed hill'.

6 After taking in the views head back down in the direction you came. The Bristol Channel will be on your left and Cheddar Reservoir on your right. On a clear day you will be able to see Glastonbury Tor away to your right.

The path to Crook Peak

Views from the trig point include Cheddar Reservoir

At the fingerpost follow the signs to King's Wood. Keep the drystone wall on your left and go straight on as the path begins to climb. The trig point on your right is another opportunity to take in the views. The path begins to drop down and you enter **King's Wood**.

7 As you enter the wood the path is tree-lined and becomes rocky underfoot. Follow the path until you reach a car park but do not enter, instead take the footpath to your right. Go through the woodland and through a five-bar gate, then follow the main path to the left. (Keep the fields on your left as you walk and ignore any path that deviates away from the edge of the woodland.) Pass through another five-bar gate. You should see glimpses of Cheddar Reservoir on your left. Where the path splits take the left-hand route that weaves downhill. Go straight over the path crossroads, following the blue arrow indicating the public bridleway.

8 Follow the path down to a gate. The footpath becomes rocky and slippery. At the foot of the hill, join Old Coach Road, turn right to walk past the White Hart pub and back to your car.

The name 'Crook Peak' may be linked to old English 'cruc' meaning 'pointed hill'

The Iron Age hill fort on Dolebury Warren

WALK 2
Dolebury Warren and Rowberrow

Start/finish	The Swan Inn, Rowberrow
Locate	///cobble.sensible.storybook
Cafes/pubs	Pub at start
Transport	No public transport
Parking	Paid parking at The Swan Inn (BS25 1QL) or limited free parking in layby 500m along Rowberrow Lane
Toilets	No public toilets on route

Once occupied by the Romans, the heathland, limestone grassland and scrub of Dolebury Warren support a variety of wildlife, including the small pearl-bordered fritillary butterfly. In the Middle Ages, the site was used as a rabbit warren and the remains of the stone Warrener's Hut can be found at the highest point of the hillfort. Combine this walk with a pub lunch at the renowned Swan Inn.

Time 2hr
Distance 6km (3.7 miles)
Climb 150m

Climb Dolebury Warren high upon the Mendip Hills, with glorious views and Iron Age fort ramparts that are fun to explore

Entering the woodland below Dolebury Warren

SHORT WALKS CHEDDAR AND THE MENDIPS

The Swan Inn, Rowberrow

1 With the pub at your back and facing the car park, turn left and take the first left along School Lane. As the lane drops downhill, take the stoney footpath on your left. At the bottom of the hill, come to a mini footpath crossroads. Cross over the farm track and go straight ahead, following the footpath into the trees. There are many paths through the woodland – stick to the lower, left-hand, options until you reach a footpath T-junction. Turn right, head uphill and continue straight ahead on this path, ignoring the entrance to Rowbarrow Warren. After a steady uphill climb through the woodland, reach a T-junction.

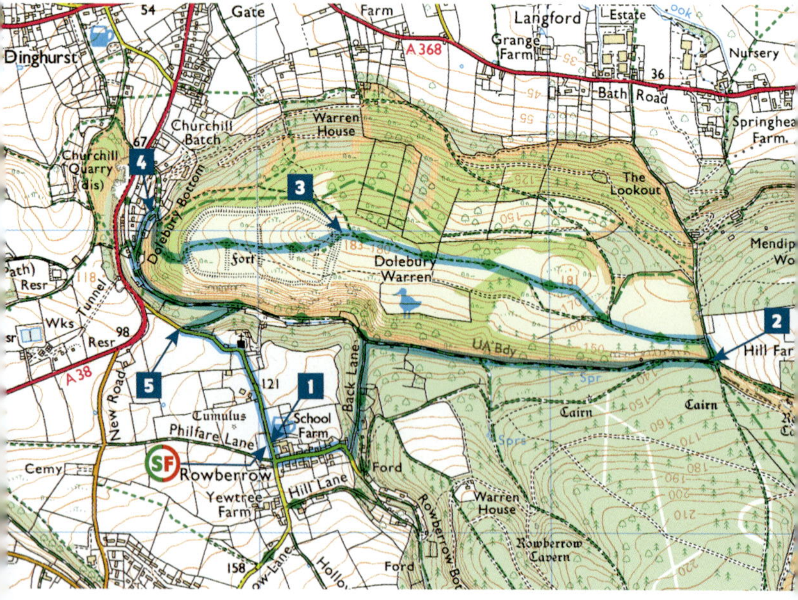

Approaching the Iron Age fort with Steep Holm island ahead

2 Turn left. After 80m or so, take the turning on your left, passing through a gate which opens out to a grassland area. Follow the path straight ahead. Go through the first set of gates on your right, and then left at the fork in the path. Go up, ignoring smaller paths diverting from the well-trodden path, until the footpath opens out to grassland. Follow the path straight ahead before entering woodland. You will now see signage for the Limestone Link and the Butcombe Trail – follow these arrows. Continue through the gates onto **Dolebury Warren**. As the path heads for the ramparts, you'll see the island of Steep Holm in the Bristol Channel straight ahead. Cross the ramparts to the Iron Age **hill fort**.

Enjoy exploring this ancient site. In summer rare butterflies are spotted here. The 'craters' in the ground that you walk past link back to the site's past, including quarrying and its use as a rabbit warren.

3 Keeping the same trajectory, walk across the middle of the hill fort towards the woodlands of **Dolebury Bottom**. To keep your bearings, keep a church below to your left while you continue ahead, rejoining the path as it enters the woodland. When the path forks after the ramparts, take the right-hand path, which is rocky. Pass through the gate with Dolebury Warren information board to your left.

SHORT WALKS CHEDDAR AND THE MENDIPS

The final climb over gnarly tree roots before you reach the pub

4 Turn left at the T-junction in the path and join the lane, passing Walnut House on your left. After passing The Oak House on your left, turn left along the lane. Continue straight ahead through the gate and enter a wooded area. The path leads ahead with a stream to your right. Keep an eye out for a footpath on the right which leads you over the stream. Go up through the woodland to a gate onto a road.

5 Take care when joining the road. Turn left towards **Rowberrow**, walking past the church on your left. The Swan Inn is a little further on your left.

WALK 3
Beacon Batch and Velvet Bottom

Start/finish	*Ubley Warren Drive, Blagdon*
Locate	*///convinced.carpeted.lunging*
Cafes/pubs	*None on route*
Transport	*No public transport*
Parking	*Free parking in layby (BS40 7XR)*
Toilets	*No public toilets on route*

Time 2hr 30min
Distance 10km
(6.2 miles)
Climb 180m

A climb to the highest point on the Mendip Hills, with Exmoor ponies roaming in a scarred, yet beautiful, landscape

From as early as the Roman times this area of the Mendip Hills has seen mining activity. The land was rich with lead and the landscape you see today bears evidence of large-scale lead extraction. Much of the valley at Velvet Bottom is designated as a Scheduled Monument. Exmoor ponies roam freely at Beacon Batch and the views are far-reaching. The climb up to Beacon Batch can be soggy underfoot, depending on the season.

The heathland area is popular with walkers, cyclists and horse-riders

The valley at Velvet Bottom bears evidence of mining activity

1 From the layby the footpath is clearly marked with a **Velvet Bottom** information board. Pass through the gate. The footpath is uneven (and can be slippery when wet) as it leads you through a landscape bearing marks of its industrial mining past. The path twists and turns but is easy to follow. After approximately 1.5km (20min) you will arrive at a large information board. Keep straight on, following the path over rocky sections before it returns to grassland underfoot. Go through the gate and turn right (do not follow the signpost to 'Cheddar via gorge') along a footpath that is rocky underfoot.

2 Enter **Long Wood Nature Reserve**. The path leads uphill. After the climb up, do not turn left but pass through the footpath gate marked as the West Mendip Way. Keep the fence on your left and walk straight ahead through the field. There are often sheep in here who are very used to walkers, but do keep dogs on leads. At the gate, turn right, join the farmer's driveway and

WALK 3 – BEACON BATCH AND VELVET BOTTOM

pass the buildings of **Charterhouse Farm** on your right. Continue along the driveway, passing a tumbledown barn on your left. At the end of the driveway cross the cattlegrid and turn left to join the road.

3 After about 0.8km (15min) walk along the road, look out for a footpath on your right. Marked as a bridleway, the path leads uphill along the side of a field and through a gate. There are three footpath options – take the path directly ahead. The path weaves through ferns – do not divert but keep following ahead until you reach a wider opening. Turn right (it can be boggy underfoot here). On reaching a

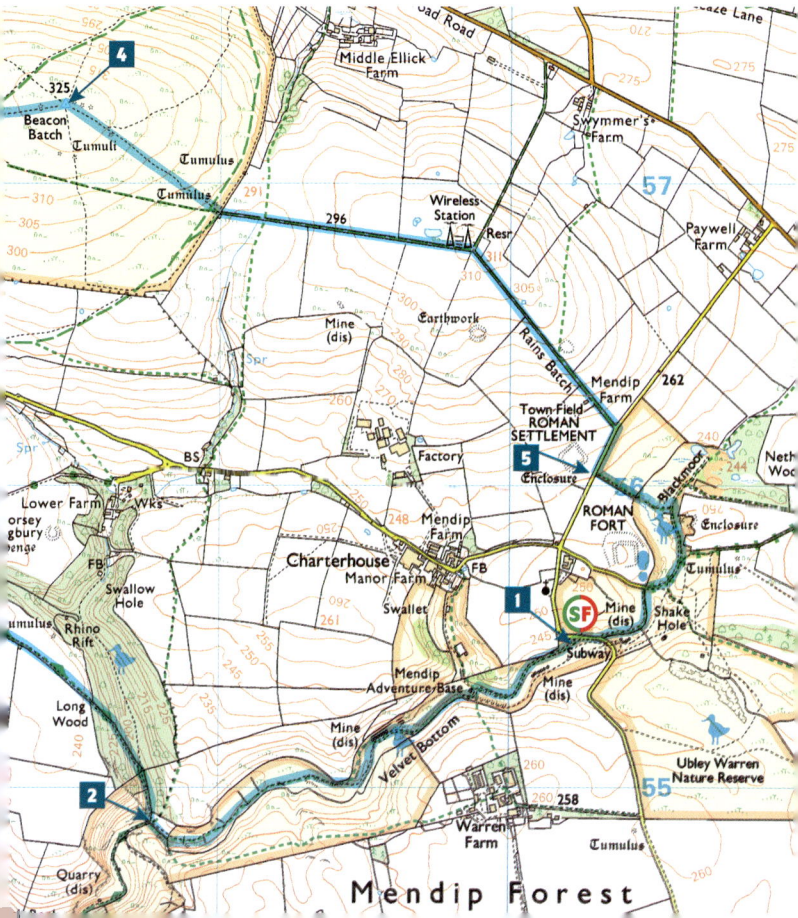

SHORT WALKS CHEDDAR AND THE MENDIPS

crossroads in the path (marked by a very short signpost) follow the bridleway straight on until the path changes to a hard pack path. Here, turn right as this is the main route to the trig point on **Beacon Batch**. At 325m high, this is the highest point on the Mendip Hills with panoramic views.

4 With the trig point behind you, follow the path downhill in the direction of the two masts ahead of you and Blagdon Lake to your left. Pass through a gate to the left of the Countryside Code information board with the two masts still ahead of you. Pass the **masts**, turn right and join the lane. At

Wild ponies roam freely on Beacon Batch

The trig point at Beacon Batch, the highest point of the Mendips

> ⓘ *Exmoor ponies are used for conservation on Mendip to help manage vegetation as they are able to graze on tough grasses and even scrub.*

the end of the lane, turn right and walk along the road for a couple minutes. Look out for the footpath to your left, in the hedge.

5 Go through the gate and walk ahead with the drystone wall on your right. Go through another gate to cross a stream before joining a footpath with dark grey stones underfoot. This is the fiddliest part of the walk. Ignore the first footpath on your right but keep an eye out for another footpath on your right, just after you have passed three trees. Weave around and up, taking the four steps on your left. Join the footpath at the top of the steps and turn right. At the car park, follow the road to your right, passing through the gate on your left. Follow the path through the ancient landscape, through a gate and arrive back at the layby where you started.

The gorge was shaped by meltwater from glaciers

WALK 4
Piney Sleights and north of Cheddar Gorge

Time 3hr
Distance 8.8km (5.5 miles)
Climb 365m

This challenging walk gives spectacular views north of the Gorge and explores ancient woodland and nature reserves

Start/finish	The Cheddar Cakery, Cheddar
Locate	///intrigues.earliest.responds
Cafes/pubs	Plenty of pubs and cafes in Cheddar village centre
Transport	Buses 48, 66, 126 and 668
Parking	Cliff Street car park (BS27 3PS)
Toilets	Cheddar village centre

Step back in time as you explore ancient inland cliff paths, protected woodlands and special nature reserves. This walk is challenging in places, with steep uneven climbs. Although it uses part of the main 'tourist' trail to see the awe-inspiring gorge, the majority of the route takes you away from the well-trodden pathways so you can experience the peacefulness of the Mendip Hills.

Pass through the wooden gate for the Gorge Walk

SHORT WALKS CHEDDAR AND THE MENDIPS

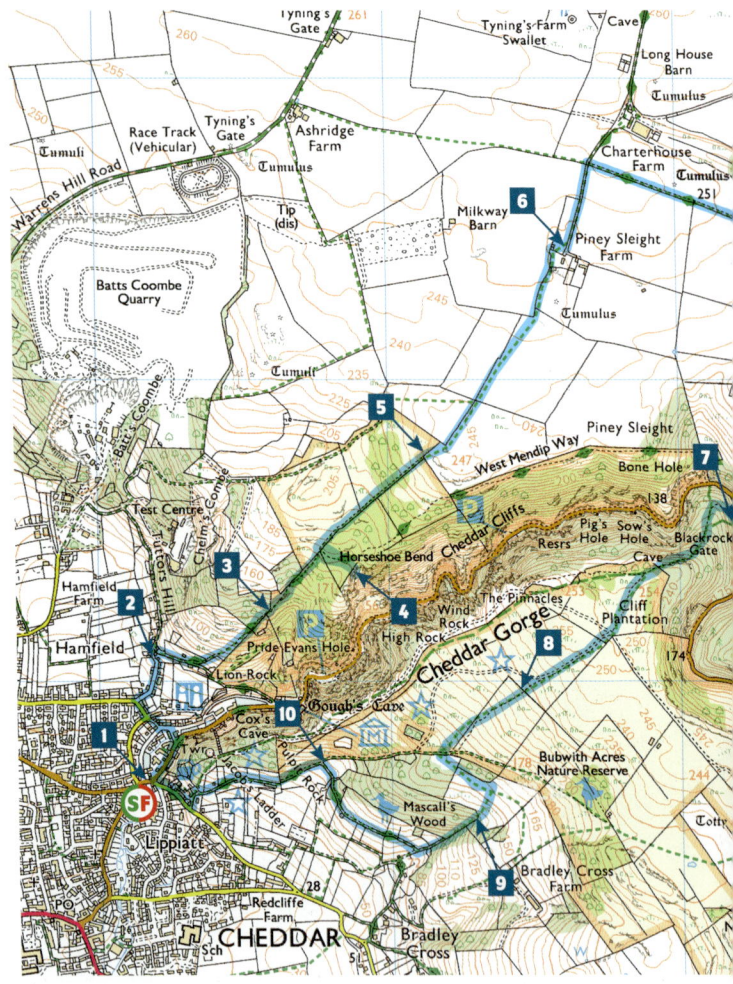

1 With The Cheddar Cakery on your left, cross the footbridge over the river, walk up through the village centre and take the road on your left called The Bays. Cross the river, pass a Greek restaurant and where the road bears left,

WALK 4 — PINEY SLEIGHTS AND NORTH OF CHEDDAR GORGE

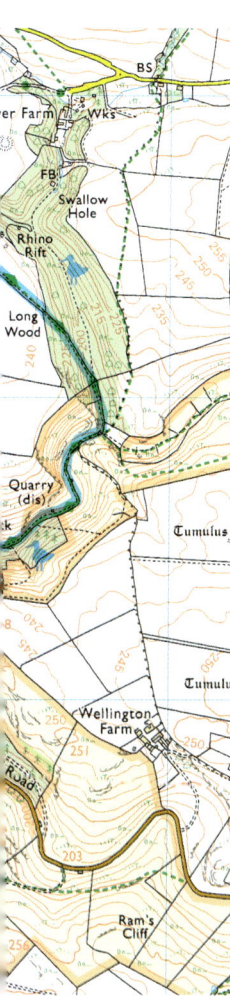

with a cream cottage called Baybrook on your right, take the small lane right immediately after the cottage. After a short, sharp climb the path joins a road. Keeping the cream cottage called Wayside on your right, go up the lane ahead, then turn right into **Tuttors Hill**. Follow the lane uphill and as it curves to the right, take a rough track on your right (marked 'Long View').

2 Follow this track and where it splits, take the left-hand path signposted 'Gorge Walk'. Pass through the gate signposted 'West Mendip Way' and head into the copse. The terrain is uneven with crumbling drystone walls on your right. Come to a footpath gate on your right.

3 Go through the gate and at a National Trust sign for Cheddar turn left, keeping the drystone wall on your left for 10m or so before the path peels away to the right. Follow the National Trust signage left for 'Gorge Walk via clifftops', go through a gate to the right, then head across the open grassland towards a gate for a short detour to take in the spectacular views over **Cheddar Gorge**.

> As you embrace the incredible views of the UK's largest inland gorge, keep an eye out for the nimble goats who cling to the cliffs! On a clear day you should be able to see across to Wales.

SHORT WALKS CHEDDAR AND THE MENDIPS

4 Retrace your steps and pass back through the rocky drystone wall where the National Trust signpost is. The next section is not signposted. With the gorge at your back, walk forwards about 5m and join a footpath to your right through gorse and ferns. Keep the crumbling drystone walls on your right and at a crossroads in the footpath continue straight ahead. As the gradient increases, the path begins to open out. You will see an intact drystone wall directly ahead with a National Trust sign for Piney Sleight and a stone stile. Before climbing the stile do pause and turn to admire the views of Cheddar Reservoir behind you.

5 Climb the stone stile and walk across the field (ignore the gate on your left). The path splits – take the left-hand fork, keeping the drystone wall on your left. Pass through the gate and walk straight ahead, now on a double track made by vehicle wheels. Go through a gateway (with no gate) into the field and continue ahead, then through another gate, with the drystone wall on your left and a hedge on your right. Clamber over the stone stile and follow the footpath ahead, then go over another stone stile beneath a large sycamore tree. Follow the footpath to the right and turn left onto the driveway for **Piney Sleight Farm**.

The stone stile and sign for Piney Sleight

Black Rock Quarry makes a good spot for a picnic

6 Follow the driveway, cross a cattlegrid and take an immediate right. Pass through the gate reconnecting you with West Mendip Way signage. Keep the drystone wall on your right, cross the field and go through a gate. The path splits here – take the left-hand fork downhill into **Long Wood Nature Reserve**. At the bottom go through a kissing gate and follow the path to the right. You are now walking through the disused Black Rock Quarry, a good spot for lunch. The path turns into a gravel track. Pass through a gate and follow signs for 'Gorge Walk. Cheddar via Clifftop south' to reach a road.

7 Cross the road to find a footpath opposite, sightly to your right, and begin the very steep, rocky ascent. At the top go through a gate and continue ahead until you reach a bench on your left and information boards on your right. Just before the bench take the grass footpath on the left (taking you away from the tourist trail). At a crossroads in the path, head straight over and up through a six-bar gate, and follow the track through the field. There are panoramic views across the county from this field. Go through the gate to enter **Bubwith Acres Nature Reserve**.

8 The path drops down, with Cheddar Reservoir seen to your right and a church directly ahead. As you descend, the path splits. Go right and walk towards an information board amongst the ferns, with a gateway on your right. Pass through the kissing gate to the right of the metal gate, continue straight down the hill for about 30m then go through another kissing gate on your left, now walking away from the reservoir. Follow the footpath through the copse, climb over a stile beneath a tree and head through ferns, keeping the bramble hedge to your right. Where the footpath splits, do not follow the path ahead to the gate in the trees but take the path that drops downhill to your right as the hedge finishes, towards **Mascall's Wood**.

9 Climb the stile and follow the obvious path through the wood. The felled trees you see hereabouts have been left to create corridors for dormice. Pass through a gate, walk downhill towards a Mascall's Wood information board then go through the kissing gate on the left. On your right a signpost with a carved owl points you in the direction of the West Mendip Way. After a slight uphill, the path flattens off and opens out to views of Cheddar on your left, then becomes a woodland walk. Continue through a gate. The path narrows and the hedges join overhead so taller walkers may need to duck. Pass through a kissing gate, turning left down the hill.

10 Continue through the gate signposted 'West Mendip Way' to join a lane into **Cheddar**. At the green shepherd's hut, turn left downhill then turn right at the T-junction. At the bottom of the hill use the footpath on the bridge to your left. The Cheddar Cakery is on your right.

The gate and information board next to Mascall's Wood

WALK 5
South of Cheddar Gorge

Time 2hr
Distance 4.5km (2.8 miles)
Climb 270m

The iconic walk with spectacular views across Cheddar Gorge

Start/finish	Edelweiss Cafe, Cheddar
Locate	///bachelor.terminology.aimed
Cafes/pubs	Plenty of pubs and cafes in Cheddar village centre
Transport	Buses 48, 66, 126, 668
Parking	Cliff Street car park (BS27 3PS)
Toilets	Cheddar village centre

Depending on the time of day, the beginning of this walk will be busy with tourists as the views are truly spectacular. But what most tourists don't know is that you'll get bonus far-reaching views when you follow this loop. There will be nimble, gravity-defying goats on this walk – get your camera ready! The terrain is rocky underfoot in places and by its very nature steep in places too.

The second half of the walk takes you away from the tourist trail

SHORT WALKS CHEDDAR AND THE MENDIPS

Cheddar Gorge, the largest gorge in the UK

1 With Edelweiss Cafe on your right and the Rasoi Kitchen and Cafe on your left, go up St Andrew's Rd and take The Lippiatt road almost immediately on the left. Head uphill and turn left into Lynch Lane, passing a green shepherd's hut on your left. Walk straight ahead (towards a set of gates for Blue Moon) and take the uneven footpath on your left.

2 Go up the path and at the top you'll find a lookout tower on your left. Turn right to go through the tall wooden gate and follow the path, keeping **Cheddar Gorge** to your left. Take time to explore the outcrop of rocks offering superior views across the gorge.

You are likely to encounter the goats of the gorge, which help manage the landscape while entertaining visitors with their gravity-defying hop, skips and jumps across the rocky cliff faces. If you visit in spring, you'll be captivated by the kids' antics.

WALK 5 – SOUTH OF CHEDDAR GORGE

As the path drops downhill, pass through another tall gate. The path splits here but rejoins later so either option is fine. A gentle stroll brings you to an information board.

3 As you approach an information board on your left, take the unmarked footpath on your right, just past a large log on your right, and follow it to a crossroads in the path.

4 Walk straight ahead through a metal gate. As the path opens out to views of Cheddar Reservoir the path forks – take the right-hand path which leads in the direction of the reservoir. Continue along the grassy path. As it descends you will lose sight of the reservoir at times. Join a stoney path, turn right and head downhill to reach a gate. Go through the gate and continue along the track.

5 On reaching the green shepherd's hut from earlier in the walk, turn left down Lynch Lane, then turn right to retrace your steps back into **Cheddar** village.

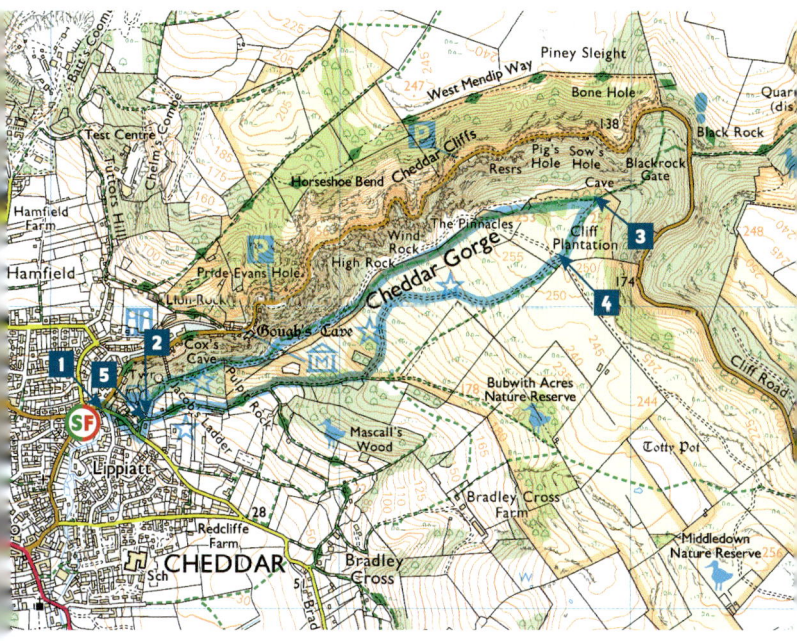

Visit in springtime and you'll be greeted with the sight of kids!

Cheddar Gorge

England's largest gorge, Cheddar Gorge was created over a million years ago in the last Ice Age by a river carving its path through the limestone rock. Today, the Cheddar Yeo river passes quietly through the centre of the village. Beneath your feet is a network of spectacular caves, some of which can be visited. These were first excavated in the 19th century. The gorge is popular with film-makers and was used as a location for *28 Years Later* (2025) and *Jack the Giant Slayer* (2013).

WALK 6
Middledown and Bubwith Acres Nature Reserves

Start/finish	The Butter Cross, Cheddar
Locate	///broom.premiums.sprinting
Cafes/pubs	Plenty of pubs and cafes in Cheddar village centre
Transport	Buses 48, 66, 126 and 668
Parking	Sainsbury's car park offers all day parking (BS27 3NZ)
Toilets	Sainsbury's

One steady climb reveals fabulous views across the Somerset Levels and Glastonbury Tor. Keep your camera to hand while exploring the nature reserves – expect to see Exmoor ponies grazing in Middledown, and you may spot rare butterflies, brown hare and, if you're lucky, peregrine falcons. Near the end of the walk you'll arrive in the main hub of Cheddar for refreshing Somerset fare, including cream teas, cider tastings, and a shop selling the only Cheddar cheese made in Cheddar!

Time 2hr
Distance 7.1km (4.4 miles)
Climb 240m

Explore two nature reserves that are home to rare plants and animals, and enjoy panoramic views across the Somerset Levels

Views across to the Somerset Levels

SHORT WALKS CHEDDAR AND THE MENDIPS

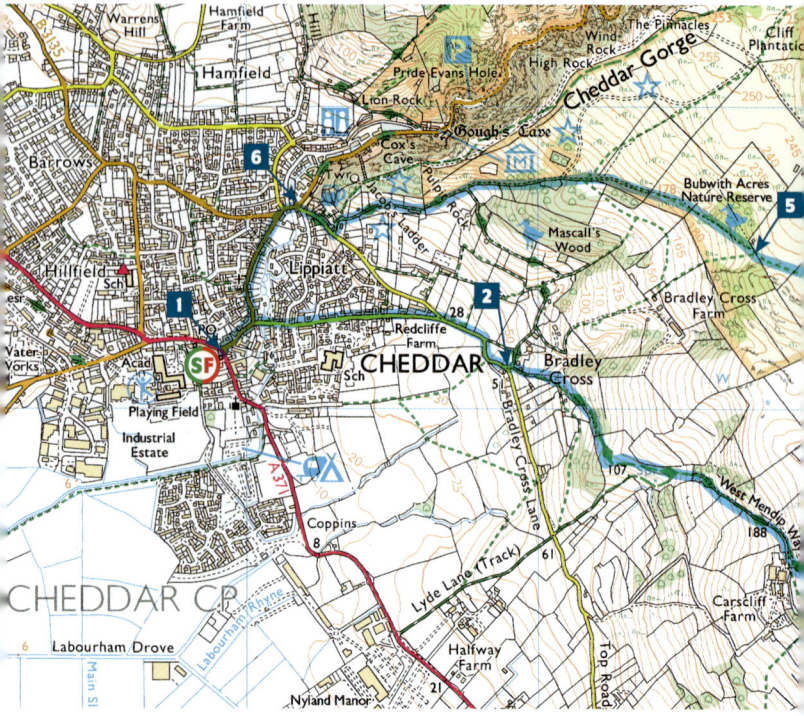

1 The 15th-century Butter Cross can be seen in the middle of the road (a triangular junction). Walk along Union Street (B3135) with the Butter Cross behind you before turning right into Redcliffe Street, crossing the **Cheddar Yeo river** by the footbridge. The residential street turns into a lane with an uphill gradient. Enjoy the views over Cheddar Reservoir as you pass a farm gate on your right.

2 A red post box on your left at **Bradley Cross** leads you to the footpath, which is a farm track. Keep the white cottage on your left, follow the track through a five-bar gate and continue through a field and another gate. As you approach a copse of trees, bear right before passing through a gateway flanked with stone pillars and with a wooden sign 'Draycott'. Take the stoney path upwards. Pass through a gate and as the path forks take the

WALK 6 – MIDDLEDOWN AND BUBWITH ACRES NATURE RESERVES

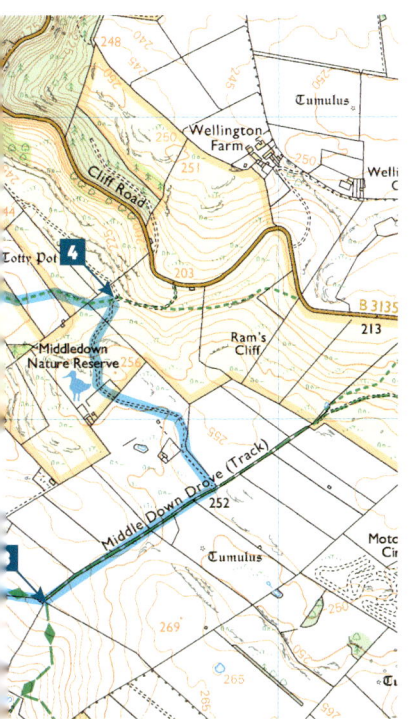

left-hand option uphill, still following the West Mendip Way. Ignore the wooden gate on your right (marked as bridleway). A double gateway adjacent to the drystone walls is ahead. Take the opportunity to stop and admire the view behind you. Pass through the gates and continue to where the path bends left.

3 The West Mendip Way continues to the right – ignore this and instead take the track (**Middle Down Drove**) to the left. After about 800m, a gateway on your left has signs for **Middledown Nature Reserve**.

Middledown Nature Reserve is known as a 'living landscape': the teams involved with preserving the 100-acre site are working together to restore, recreate and reconnect wildlife habitats.

Exmoor ponies grazing in Middledown Nature Reserve

SHORT WALKS CHEDDAR AND THE MENDIPS

Keeping the fence line on your right, follow the path through the reserve. As the path descends, take the less-walked path on your left (if you reach a padlocked gate you've gone 100m too far).

4 You will see a gate ahead – do not go through this but instead walk past the sheep dip area and keep the fence to your right until you come to a gate. Cross this field, pass a water hole on your left and head for the next gate.

5 Walk in the direction of the reservoir where a stile welcomes you to **Bubwith Acres Nature Reserve**.

Bubwith Acres Nature Reserve comprises 47 acres of unimproved grassland, scrubland and woodland. Part of the site is a Site of Special Scientific Interest (SSSI) and due to its unique nature, you will see rare plants and butterflies.

Cattle posing in front of the panoramic view

WALK 6 – MIDDLEDOWN AND BUBWITH ACRES NATURE RESERVES

The iconic 15th-century Butter Cross in Cheddar

Go through a kissing gate, following the footpath downhill in the direction of the reservoir (ignore the footpaths diverting left and right). This is a relatively steep descent, so take care on the loose gravel. When the footpath joins a lane (Lynch Lane), turn left and walk downhill before turning right down the road back towards **Cheddar**.

6 Turn right to explore the shops and eateries. To head back to the start turn left. Take care at the junction, cross the river and keep left at the mini roundabout (Tweentown Junction), following signs for Cheddar village along Cliff Street (B3135). Pass a car park on your left and then Cheddar Methodist Church on your right. The road bears to the right. Retrace your steps from earlier as you head back towards the Butter Cross.

✚ To lengthen

At Waypoint 3 turn right and follow the West Mendip Way through Draycott Sleights Nature Reserve until you reach New Road, then retrace your steps and turn right to continue the walk. This adds around 3km (1hr).

Axbridge architecture dates from the 15th century

WALK 7
Cheddar Reservoir and Axbridge

Start/finish	*Axbridge Town car park*
Locate	*///irony.seaweed.robots*
Cafes/pubs	*Pub and tea rooms in Axbridge*
Transport	*Buses 48, 62, 66 and 126*
Parking	*Axbridge Town car park (BS26 2BG)*
Toilets	*Moorland Street, Axbridge*

Time 1hr 30min
Distance 5km (3.1 miles)
Climb 25m

A mainly flat walk round Cheddar Reservoir, with a backdrop of Cheddar Wood and views across farmland

Although Cheddar Reservoir was built in 1937, it was only during the 1980s that the public were fully permitted to walk around it. Keen birdwatchers will spot chiffchaff, goldcrest, linnet and reed bunting. There are several refreshment options in Axbridge, although the wall around the reservoir also makes a great spot for a picnic, and there's an interesting museum in the town centre.

Cheddar Reservoir is popular for watersports

SHORT WALKS CHEDDAR AND THE MENDIPS

The wall around the reservoir is a good spot for a picnic

1 With the car park behind you, turn left along Old Church Road. Pass the pharmacy on your right and turn right down Moorland Street, passing the public toilets and drinking fountain. Follow this road which soon becomes a track. Do not let the sign 'No Access to Reservoir' put you off your stride. Turn left, keep the stream on your left and follow the track (**Portmeade Drove**) as it bends to the right (do not enter the gates on the bend).

2 Continue along Portmeade Drove, keeping an eye out on your left for a gate to access the land surrounding the reservoir. Follow the track through the field. There is a small stile (not dog friendly) on the left which will take you up to the top of **Cheddar Reservoir**. If you wish to avoid the stile (or have a dog) continue through the field to a gate. Turn left and after about 20m you will see a turning circle and large oak trees on your left. Go through the gate

WALK 7 – CHEDDAR RESERVOIR AND AXBRIDGE

beneath the tree and up the grass bank to the reservoir.

3 On reaching the reservoir, turn right, keep the water on your left and walk anti-clockwise around the reservoir. Go through the gate next to the pumping tower, pass a car park, skate park, sports pitches and finally the **yacht club** on your right. You will see a five-bar gate and kissing gate ahead – do not pass through these but instead

> ⓘ *Cheddar Reservoir is one of the best places to spot waterbirds such as coots, pochards, and the great northern diver.*

walk down the tarmac access road and turn left through a gate.

4 With the gate behind you, the reservoir to your left and **Cheddar Wood** to your right, walk straight ahead to

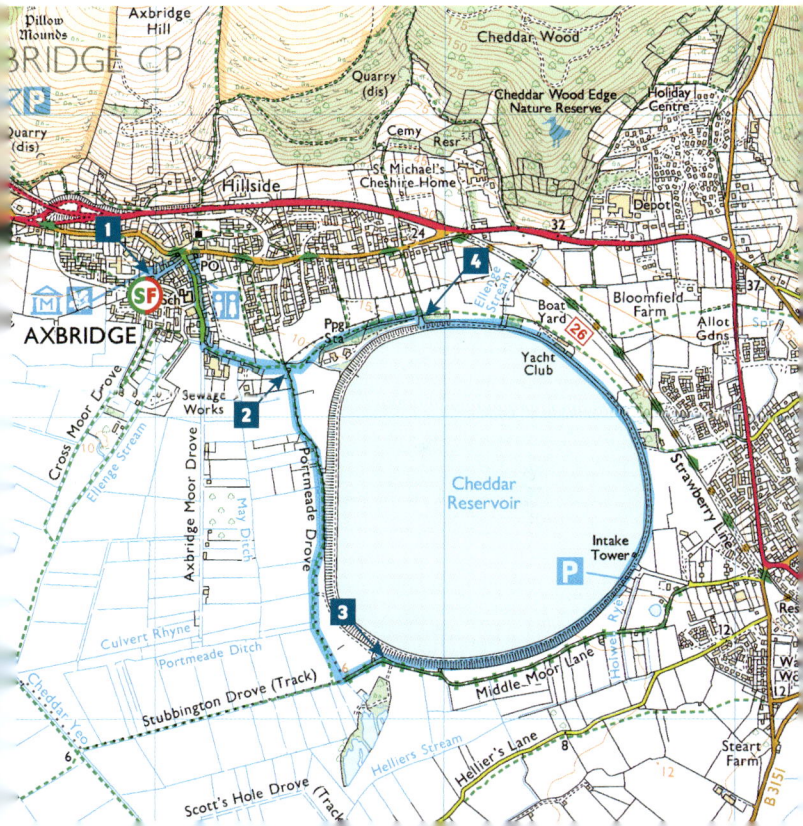

After the reservoir the footpath leads through a copse

join the well-trodden footpath. Stroll through the copse and into the field. and follow the tracks to a gate on your left. Cross the stream and continue through the next field past a derelict barn on your left. Go through gates to rejoin Portmeade Drove. With the stream on your right, now retrace your steps back along the track to the start. Turn right at the end of the track and head up to Axbridge town centre to visit the tea room, pubs, church or museum.

St John the Baptist Church in Axbridge is dog friendly

King John's Hunting Lodge

King John's Hunting Lodge on the Square in Axbridge

Axbridge town square is dominated by the very handsome building of King John's Hunting Lodge. The name is misleading as the Tudor Lodge was built as a wool-merchant's house in 1500 and King John was crowned in 1199! None the less, the building is striking and is home to the Axbridge and District Museum, open from April to October (Tuesday to Sunday 1pm-4pm). The exhibitions focus on the Axbridge and Mendip Hills area and provide historical insights into life here over the ages (www.kingjohnshuntinglodge.co.uk).

This flat walk goes through working farmland

WALK 8
Rhynes and droves

Start/Finish	*Cheddar Reservoir car park (south)*
Locate	*///easygoing.beside.prominent*
Cafes/pubs	*None on route*
Transport	*No public transport*
Parking	*Cheddar Reservoir car park (south) (BS27 2LH)*
Toilets	*No public toilets on route*

Although the Mendip Hills are touching distance away, this peaceful, flat walk embraces the serenity of the immediate lowlands. The walk begins with a longish stretch along quiet country lanes; take your binoculars and enjoy sightings of deer, swans and birdlife in the fields away from any hustle and bustle. There's an option to climb up to join the reservoir circuit at the end.

Time 2hr
Distance 9km (5.6 miles)
Climb 0m

Some days you just want an easy peaceful stroll and this lowland walk offers just that

Grasses, sedges and rushes flank the rhynes, providing a rich habitat for wildlife

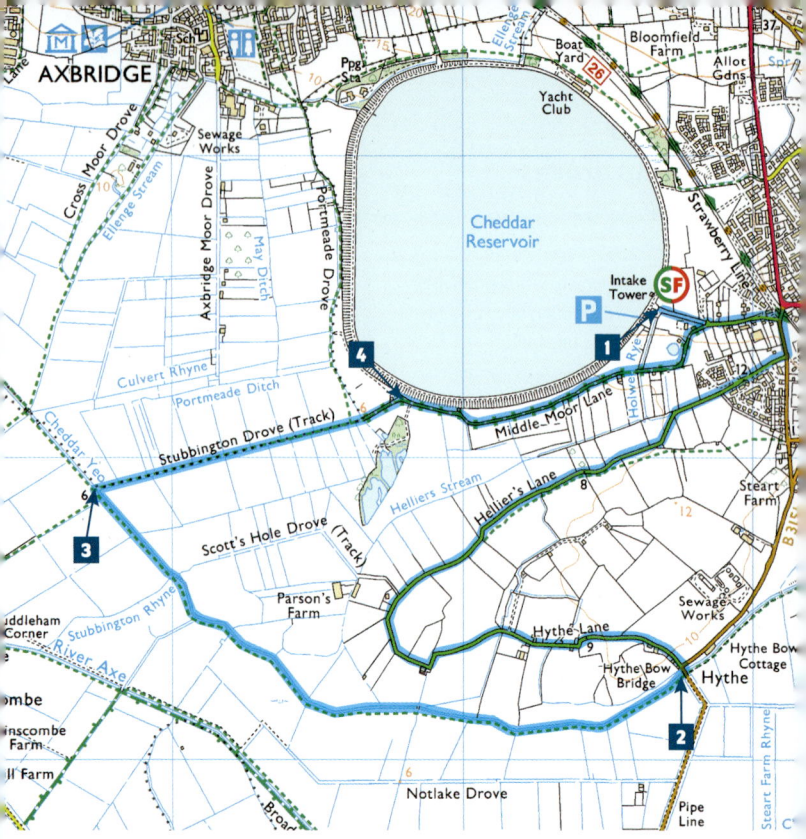

1 With Cheddar Reservoir at your back and the Sharpham Road playing fields on your left, walk down the tree-lined driveway. Continue ahead along the road, turning right at the T-junction. Walk along the road with care before taking the first turning on your right into **Hellier's Lane**. Follow this quiet residential lane straight ahead. Expect to see flocks of birds in the fields, especially starlings in winter. After approximately 40min (3km) of strolling, come to a T-junction.

2 Turn right to cross **Hythe Bow Bridge** and take the footpath on your right immediately after the bridge. Walk along the edge of the field with the rhyne on your right. Much of the county is very low and these rhynes (man-made ditches or canals) help drain the wetlands into usable pasture.

WALK 8 – RHYNES AND DROVES

Pass through a succession of metal gates (13 if all closed!) with the Mendip Hills as a stunning backdrop.

3 After passing a large metal pipe which crosses over the rhyne, turn right over the footbridge and join the hedge-lined **Stubbington Drove**. (This can be very wet and muddy in winter.) Continue straight ahead along the droveway. Droveways are historical routes which were used by farmers to move their livestock, on foot, between grazing lands and pastures, or to take them to market. As the droveway begins to bend to the right, there is a turning circle beneath oak trees on your left.

For an alternative route with a view of the reservoir, pass through the

There is an option to join the pathway along the top of Cheddar Reservoir

small footpath gate beneath the trees and climb up the grassy bank. Turn right at the top to head back in the direction of the car park.

4 If you'd rather keep to the flat, continue along the **Middle Moor Lane**, keeping the reservoir away to your left. As the lane ends, it rejoins the driveway to the car park.

Looking back along the rhyne with views of the Mendip Hills

Ashton Windmill, a rare sight for Somerset

WALK 9
Ashton Windmill

Time 1hr
Distance 3.7km (2.3 miles)
Climb 40m

Step back in time to Somerset's rural heritage with a short windmill and willow walk

Start/finish	Ashton Windmill, Chapel Allerton, near Wedmore
Locate	///year.highlight.soup
Cafes/pubs	None on route
Transport	No public transport
Parking	At Ashton Windmill (BS28 4QF)
Toilets	No public toilets on route

Somerset is renowned for its wetlands, which make perfect growing conditions for withy beds. If you do this walk between May and October you'll see willow rods reaching over 2.5m high, to be used by local basket weavers. The Ashton Windmill is one of only two in the county and makes the perfect spot for a picnic with views. It is usually open to visitors on a Sunday (April to September) but best to check ahead by calling the Friends of Ashton Windmill on 01278 789859.

The willow crop may alter the position of footpaths

The walk crosses the field towards Brent Knoll hill in the distance

1 After entering the grounds of **Ashton Windmill**, take a left, walk to the bottom corner of the paddock and climb the stile.

> Built between 1766 and 1774, Ashton Windmill is an old flour mill which stands on a ridge called the 'Isle of Wedmore'. The mill was last working in 1927 but there has been windmill on the site since 1317.

Keeping the hedge to your left, walk around the field and through the working farmyard. Turn right along the lane, walking slightly uphill. The footpath is on your left through a gate (opposite Ashton Mill Farm). Take the second gateway on your left, turning right through the field to the stile ahead. Keeping the hedge to your left, continue straight on through a five-bar gate. With the hedge now to your right, pass through the two footpath gates in the corner of the field, ignoring the rusty brown gateway on your left.

2 Cross the field in the direction of Brent Knoll (the bumpy hill in the distance), and you'll see the churchyard emerging. Cross the stile directly opposite the entrance to Allerton Church. Turn left along the road, walking past **Manor Farm** on your right. Continue over the crossroads and follow the road straight on, signposted 'Unsuitable for long vehicles'.

WALK 9 – ASHTON WINDMILL

3 Pass Moorland Farm on your left, then take the grassy track on your right (just before Little Moorland Farm Lodge). This footpath is labelled **Copeswood Lane** on OS Maps and can get very wet underfoot. After walking past a five-bar gate on your left, take the footpath on your right. Follow it up the field, bearing slightly right. Keep the house and outbuildings to your left and exit via a five-bar gate. Turn left onto the lane and just before **Brook House Farm**, go through the footpath gate on your right.

4 Cross the paddock straight ahead and go through two consecutive gates. Depending on the time of year you may be greeted by very high willow rods! (Note – the willow crop alters the positioning of the footpaths shown on the OS map.) At this point, keep the hedge to your left and follow the path

> ⓘ *Somerset boasts a rich heritage of willow weaving due to the unique wetland environment on the Levels.*

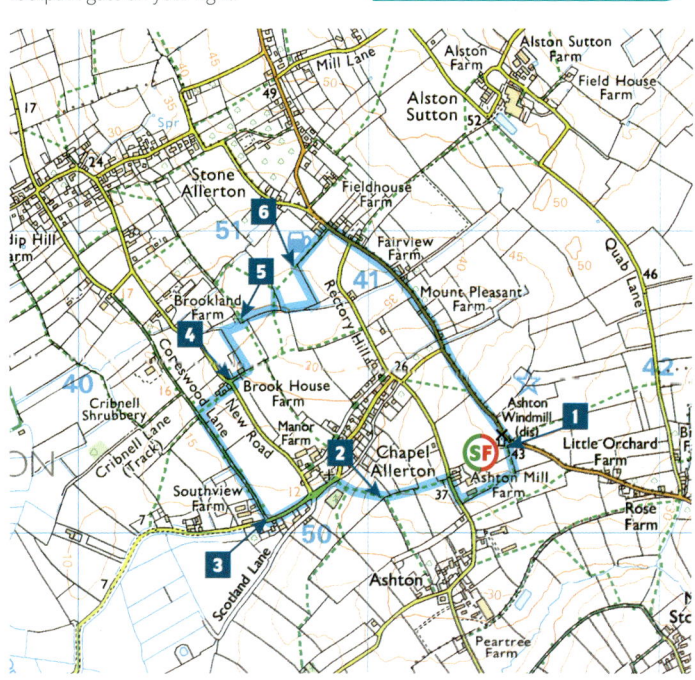

The mill was last working in 1927

around the field until you reach a gap in the hedge opposite an ash tree.

5 Cross the stream into the next field. Keep right with the stream to your right then bear left, keeping the hedge on your right. Turn right through the next gap in the hedge, keeping the hedge to your right. Ignore the gateway on your right, but continue towards a large oak tree in the middle distance. On reaching the oak tree you'll see that it is in fact three trees!

6 Follow the path as it bends to the right behind the trees and walk towards the white properties in the distance. Pass through the gate onto the road. Turn right and follow the road back towards **Chapel Allerton** and the windmill.

WALK 10
Nyland Hill

Time 2hr
Distance 5.3km (3.3 miles)
Climb 90m

A short sharp climb to a trig point takes in panoramic views across Somerset

Start/finish	Strawberry Special Inn, Station Road, Draycott
Locate	///increment.holdings.boomer
Cafes/pubs	Pub at start (check opening hours online)
Transport	Bus 126 to Draycott (limited service)
Parking	Limited on-road parking opposite pub (BS27 3TQ)
Toilets	No public toilets on route

Follow sleepy country lanes past numerous farms before climbing Nyland Hill to delight in 360-degree views across Cheddar, the Mendip Hills and beyond to the Somerset coast. You can expect to see horses, cattle and apple trees as you experience a walk through a traditional farming community.

Lush green Somerset fields

Views across Cheddar, the Mendip Hills and beyond

WALK 10 – NYLAND HILL

1 With the pub on your right walk along Station Road, taking the first left into Milking Lane and then an immediate right along Hardmead Lane. Pass through a kissing gate with stables on your right, go through a gate along the side of the paddocks and then through a footpath gate. Cross the field straight ahead aiming for a five-bar gate and footpath gate.

2 Turn left onto **Latches Lane**, passing Moormead Farm buildings on your right. Enjoy the rural landscape either side of this lane, with cattle in fields and farmers at work. Follow the lane as it passes Court Farm and Batts Farm and curves right past Crane Farmhouse on your left and then New House Farm. Continue along the lane, passing Decoy Pool Farm, then Nyland Coach House on your left. Look out for a footpath on your left just after some red-topped gate posts (opposite Tor Farm Lodges on the right).

3 Go through the five-bar gate and follow the track up the hill. After passing through another gate, look left for the track which leads to the trig point at the top of **Nyland Hill**. On a clear day you can see as far as Glastonbury Tor in one direction and the Somerset coast in another. (If you don't wish to climb to the top, follow the footpath round the lower levels of the hill and rejoin the route further on.)

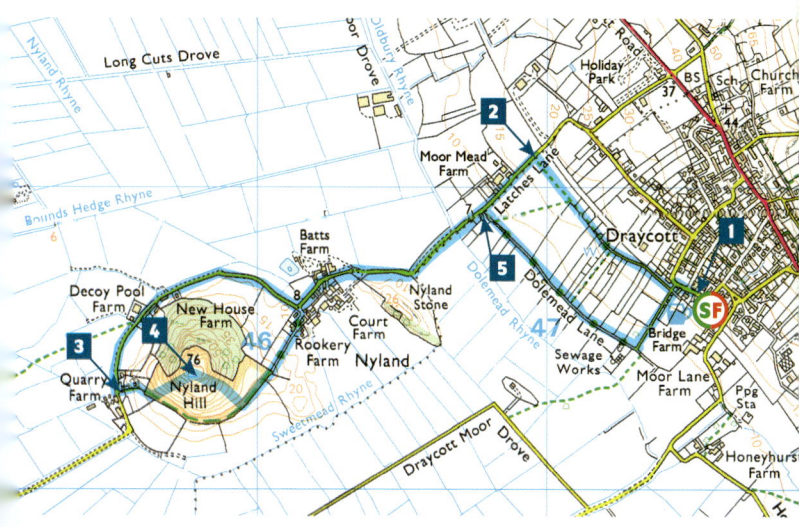

It's a sharp climb to the trig point, but the views are worth the effort

4 With Cheddar Reservoir and the trig point at your back, Glastonbury Tor directly ahead, make your way down the hill, turning left once you rejoin the lower path. Go through the gates into a hedge-lined track with **Rookery Farm** on your left. Follow the lane to the left before turning right, past the red post box in the wall on your right, retracing some of your steps from earlier.

5 Immediately after passing a brown and white stable on your right, take the

gravel lane on your right (marked as **Dolemead Lane** on the OS map). As the lane bears left into Milking Lane, a brook babbles on your right. At the end of the lane turn right (signposted 'Strawberry Line') and the pub will be on your left.

> ⓘ *Many years ago, Nyland Hill would have been 'an island' in the Somerset landscape, standing proud in the once flooded marshes.*

A true 'Mendip' view with a typical drystone wall in the foreground

WALK 11
Westbury-sub-Mendip

Start/finish	*Westbury-sub-Mendip Post Office, Stoke Road*
Locate	*///verges.ordinary.crows*
Cafes/pubs	*Pub in Westbury*
Transport	*Bus 126 (limited service)*
Parking	*In layby on Stoke Road (BA5 1HD)*
Toilets	*No public toilets on route*

Time 2hr 30min
Distance 5.6km (3.5 miles)
Climb 210m

You can't beat Somerset strawberries and this walk explores this unique part of the county's heritage

A walk of two halves. Begin with a steady climb through a nature reserve for rewarding panoramic views across the county before wandering along the level Strawberry Line, a dual-use path for cyclists and walkers which follows the track of the old Cheddar Valley railway once used to transport locally grown strawberries to London and Birmingham.

The view back from the entrance to Lynchcombe Nature Reserve

SHORT WALKS CHEDDAR AND THE MENDIPS

1 With the Westbury-sub-Mendip Post Office at your back, turn left up School Hill, past the war memorial, school and Old Vicarage on your right. Take the road on your right, pass Phoenix Cottage on your right and walk along Top Road. Bear left at Back Lane but immediately walk straight ahead signposted 'Perch Hill which leads to Lynchcombe Lane'. Ignore the turning on the right for Perch Hill and continue along **Lynchcombe Lane**, which turns into a rough farm track. Continue along and up, ignoring all other gates until you reach a footpath gate with a nature reserve information board on your left.

2 Enter **Lynchcombe Nature Reserve** and follow the footpath through the field, then go through the five-bar gate marked as a bridleway with a blue sign. (Keep dogs on a lead here between April and Sept as

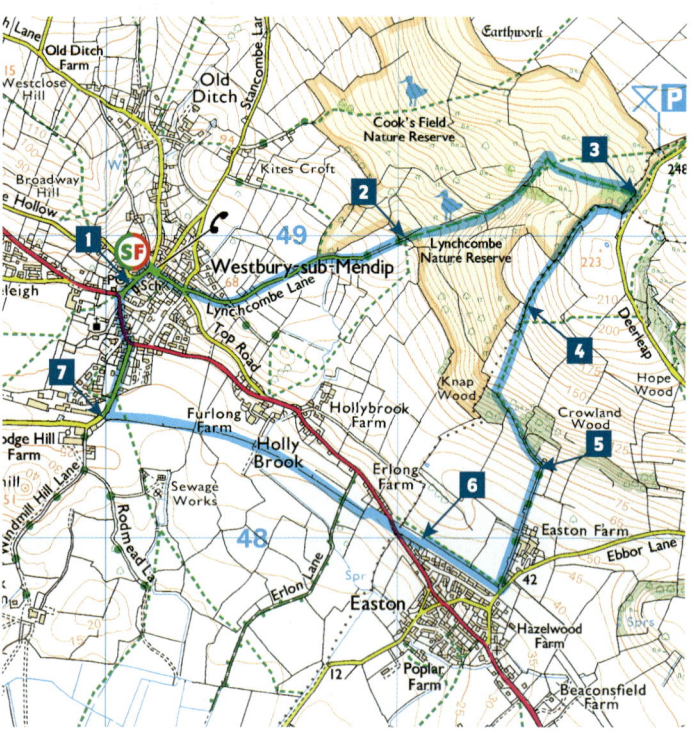

WALK 11 – WESTBURY-SUB-MENDIP

The walk passes a red-tiled barn

skylarks nest on the ground.) Follow the path uphill and bear right as you near the top. Keep eyes right for views of Glastonbury Tor on the horizon. Reach a gate and go through.

3 Take the footpath immediately on your right, keeping a drystone wall on your right. Do not cross the road ahead. The footpath leads through a copse to a stile. Climb the stile and continue ahead, keeping a drystone wall on your right. On a clear day you can see across to the Bristol Channel and the island of Steep Holm. The path naturally leads around the edge of the field and then a copse. Go through a gate and walk straight ahead with a drystone wall on your right.

4 Walk past a red-tiled barn on your right. Over to your left is a dew pond between two stone walls. Keep the fence line on your right and continue downhill. After a water trough on your right, the footpath hugs the fence before dropping down into a gully. Climb over the stile to the left of a gate. The footpath joins a lane at Crowland Coppice.

5 Head down the hill. Just before the lane meets the road, go through the gate on your right to join the

SHORT WALKS CHEDDAR AND THE MENDIPS

The Strawberry Line dual-use path

ⓘ *The area around Cheddar is renowned for its strawberries, mainly grown on the south-facing slopes of the Mendip Hills.*

Strawberry Line. The path curves to the left at a bench.

The Strawberry Line is under continual transformation as a group of volunteers work to create an accessible path to connect the coastal town of Clevedon with Shepton Mallet via Cheddar. With regular sections being opened, check out www. thestrawberryline.org.uk for the latest map information.

6 Go past the bench on your left, walk beneath a traffic bridge and through archways. Continue ahead, cross over a lane and on past another bench nestled under an archway on your right. As the path bends to the right, you will pass a wildlife area on your left with picnic bench. Continue along the Strawberry Line until you join a road on the outskirts of **Westbury-sub-Mendip**.

7 Turn right, passing Bell Close on your right to reach a T-junction. Turn left, pass the Westbury Inn on your right and follow the pavement back to the war memorial and Post Office.

WALK 12
Ebbor Gorge and Ebbor Wood

Start/finish	Ebbor Gorge National Nature Reserve
Locate	///hint.inserted.lunching
Cafes/pubs	None on route
Transport	No public transport
Parking	Ebbor Gorge National Nature Reserve car park (BA5 1AY)
Toilets	No public toilets on route

Time 1hr 30min
Distance 2.5km (1.6 miles)
Climb 135m

A short walk surrounded by ferns and woodland, and a rocky scramble through the heart of an ancient gorge

Although this walk is short in distance, parts of it are challenging. Begin with an enchanting woodland walk before scrambling over rocks through an ancient gorge. Ebbor Gorge National Nature Reserve is of geological interest and there is evidence of Stone and Bronze Age human activity. The path through the woods can be muddy and the rocks of the gorge uneven and slippery after rain.

The ancient woodland feels atmospheric

Enjoy walking through the ancient gorge

WALK 12 – EBBOR GORGE AND EBBOR WOOD

1 With the car park behind you and the Ebbor Gorge Information Station to your right, follow the footpath up through the trees. The path soon splits; take the left-hand option and follow the path through **Ebbor Wood**.

> Ebbor Gorge began to be formed approximately 2 million years ago and it is believed humans first arrived in Britain 1 million years ago. An early human species called *Homo heidelbergensis* was found in caves nearby.

On reaching a kissing gate, signs indicate you are leaving the nature reserve and entering a working farm. Follow the footpath up the slope into a field (there may be electric livestock fencing in place) and walk straight ahead to enter a copse of trees. Keep to the well-trodden path and come to a five-bar gate. Do not go through but follow the yellow footpath arrow pointing left and uphill. Keep the fence on your right and pass through the kissing gate at the top. Once in the field, the path bears right. Keep the fence to your right and come to two kissing gates.

2 Go through, following the same path to enter 'Ebbor Gorge Top Entrance North' marked by signs. Take the path on your right and drop down

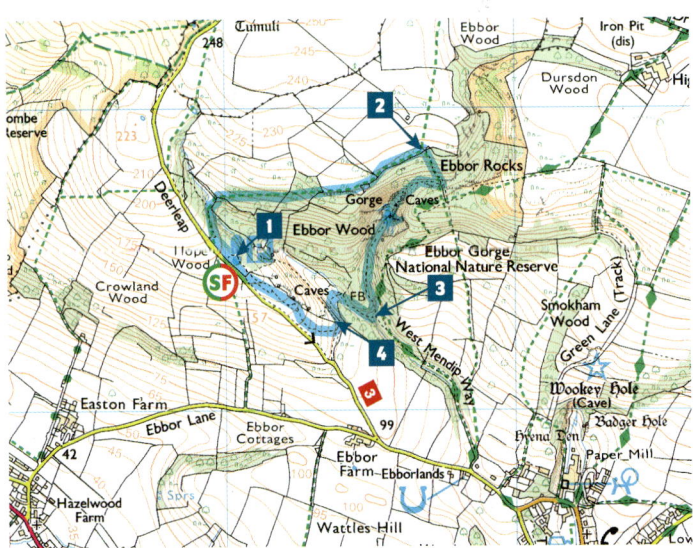

75

Far-reaching views from the top of Ebbor Gorge

the rocky path to a crossroads. Follow signs right to the viewing point, now entering **Ebbor Gorge**. The path is uneven and challenging, particularly following rain. Walking through this ancient gorge and landscape, you can easily imagine dinosaurs roaming here! Continue along the path, passing scree on your left, to reach a T-junction in the path.

A perfectly placed bench for admiring the view

3 Take the path heading right, following signs to the car park. Don't miss the metalwork animal sculpture on your right amongst the trees. Cross over the footbridge and follow the gravel path up to your left, going through a kissing gate at the top.

4 Follow signs pointing right for the car park, via steps. A path leads to a viewing area on your right marked by a stone inlaid with a brass plaque. Pass a series of benches facing the most wonderful view across the Mendip Hills and Somerset Levels, before the path links back to the car park.

WALK 13
Priddy and Deer Leap

Start/finish	*Priddy Green, Coxton End Lane*
Locate	*///stick.swerving.helps*
Cafes/pubs	*Pub in Priddy*
Transport	*No public transport*
Parking	*Free parking at Priddy Green (BA5 3BB)*
Toilets	*No public toilets on route*

Set off from the historical village of Priddy, a community which celebrates its farming heritage, and make your way through farmland to the knock-out vistas at Deer Leap. Choose a clear day for this – the views are mesmerising.

Time 2hr
Distance 6.5km (4 miles)
Climb 85m

A stroll around the peaceful village of Priddy and an unrivalled vista across the Somerset Levels

This walk includes several stone stiles

There are benches at Deer Leap for enjoying the views

1 After parking at the village green, walk past the red telephone box (with defibrillator) on your right. Turn right at the triangle in the road and pass the Queen Victoria Inn on your right. Continue along the road, passing **Ebborways Farm B&B** on your right. The footpath is on the left-hand side of the road opposite the entrance to Ebborways Farm Campsite. Go through the kissing gate. Keeping the drystone wall on your left, follow the footpath around two sides of the field and go through the next kissing gate. Cross the field, climb over a stone stile and turn right. Follow the path until you reach a T-junction.

2 Turn right to join a farm track, passing farm buildings and a bungalow on your right. Turn left when you meet a road. On a clear day you will see Glastonbury Tor in the distance on your left. Walk along the road (marked as **Pelting Drove** on the OS map) for approximately 500m, then

WALK 13 – PRIDDY AND DEER LEAP

take the clearly marked footpath on your right that leads to the car park at **Deer Leap**, where there are benches.

3 After enjoying the view, head through the gate (on your right as you approached the car park earlier), following the footpath across the grassland up towards the next gate. You are entering **Cook's Field Nature Reserve**.

Cook's Field is an 85-acre nature reserve and Site of Special Scientific Interest (SSSI). The flower-rich unimproved grasslands here have allowed rare plants to thrive, including the unusual Autumn lady's-tresses and adder's-tongue fern.

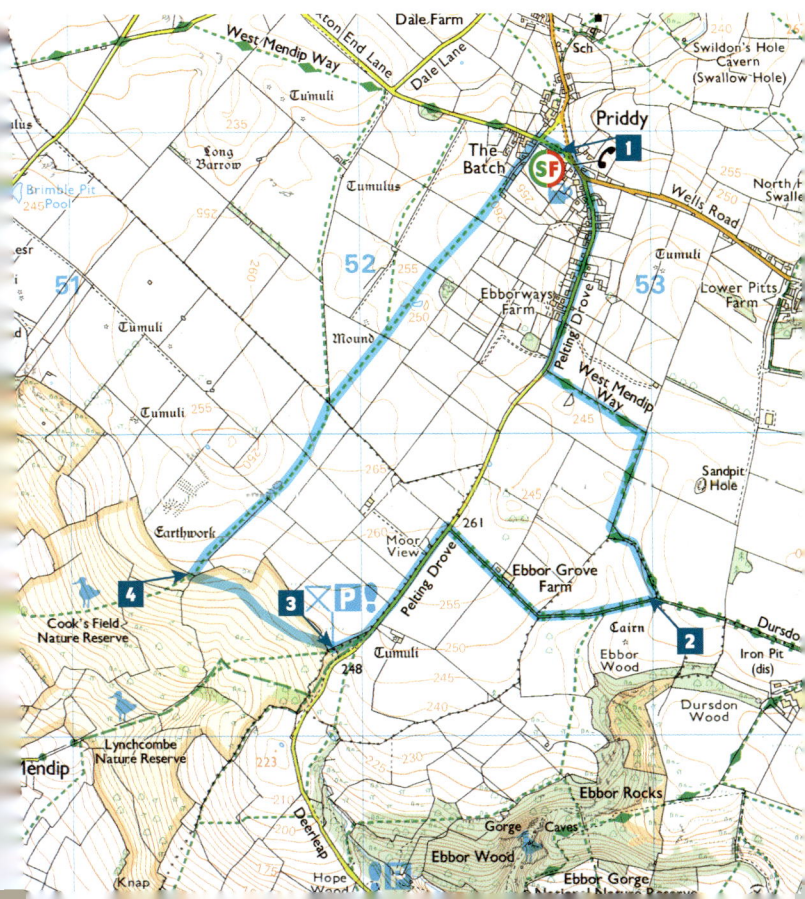

The thatched hurdle stack on Priddy Green

4 Unless you choose to explore the nature reserve, turn immediately right through the footpath gate on your right. The path leads you in a relatively straight line ahead through the next seven fields, over stone stiles and through gates. As you enter the final field, keep the farm barn and the drystone wall on your right. Climb the stile and follow the lane back to the village green where you will see the Sheep Hurdle Stack.

> ⓘ *It is believed that humans have lived in Priddy since the Neolithic times.*

✚ To lengthen

On reaching Cook's Field Nature Reserve at Waypoint 4 you can explore the nature reserve, looping back to continue the walk. There are several paths to follow while exploring the unique plant life.

Priddy Hurdle Stack

In 1348 the very first sheep fair took place on Priddy's village green. The fair was originally held in Wells, but the city was in the grip of the Black Death so the fair was moved to Priddy and stayed there until just after World War 2. It is believed that if the hurdles for the sheep pens were not stacked on site from one sheep fair until the next, the lord of the manor could refuse the right to hold the fair. The thatched hurdle stack on the village green stands as a reminder of this key part of Somerset heritage. Since 1991, the Priddy Folk Festival has used the iconic village green for a relaxed weekend of live music and camping, raising money for local charities and community groups.

The barrows are a prominent landmark at the top of North Hill

WALK 14
Priddy Nine Barrows and Stockhill Wood

Start/finish	*Stockill Wood car park*
Locate	*///plums.writings.universally*
Cafes/pubs	*None on route*
Transport	*No public transport*
Parking	*Stockill Wood car park (BA5 3AS)*
Toilets	*No public toilets on route*

The landscape here feels very different to other areas of the Mendip Hills. From the rich coniferous woodland of Stockhill (a favoured place of the elusive nightjar) to the top of North Hill with its Bronze Age burial chambers and Roman mines, this unique walk takes you away for moments of peaceful reflection.

Time 1hr 30min
Distance 5.8km (3.6 miles)
Climb 80m

Retrace the footsteps of our ancestors as you explore ancient landmarks and peaceful woodlands

The Priddy Mineries Nature Reserve next to Stockhill Wood

SHORT WALKS CHEDDAR AND THE MENDIPS

1 Walk out of the car park and cross the road. A well-trodden path is directly ahead and takes you through the Priddy Mineries Nature Reserve. Although this is a haven for wildlife today, the scene would have been very different in the Victorian era when the site was an active lead works. Bear left to follow the path until you reach the large pool, **Fair Lady Well**, on your left.

2 The next part of the route is tricky to navigate. Turn back around on yourself so that the pond is now on your right. Take the footpath on your left which leads towards mature trees, looking for a drystone wall ahead. Keep the wall on your left and follow the footpath which weaves through scrubby and tufty land uphill. Go through the gate signed 'Waldegrave Farms' and continue uphill, still

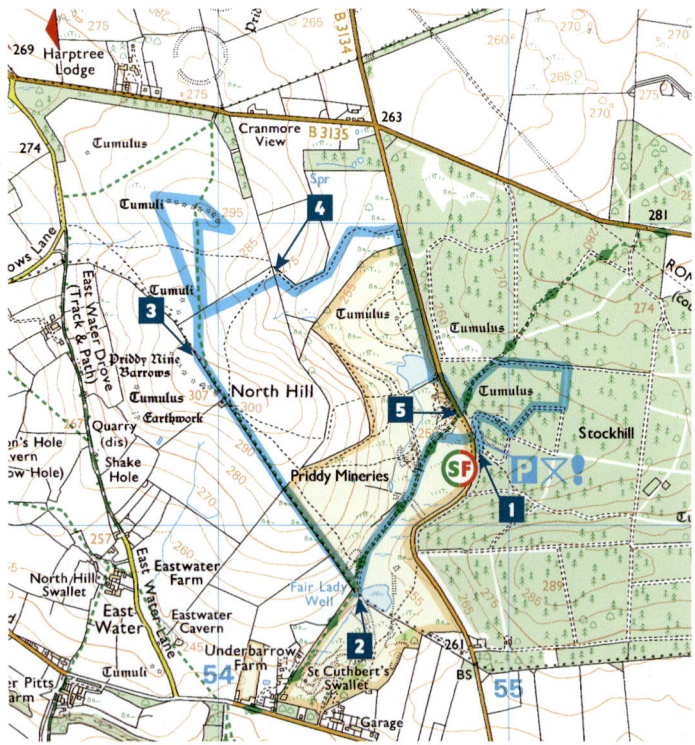

The barrows are found in fields used today for agricultural purposes

keeping the wall to your left, to the top of the **North Hill**. You will see six barrows on your left, but these are on private land.

3 To explore some of the barrows, take the footpath to your right (opposite the gate marked private land) across the field. Cross the stile and walk out and around the barrows before returning to the stile and crossing back over. Turn left, keeping the fence line to your left. You will come to a number of gates and sheep hurdles ahead.

4 Go through the small gate marked with a green and white arrow as a permissive bridleway. Take the obvious footpath ahead, passing a water trough on your left. The path drops downhill and leads you to a gate onto the road. Turn right to walk with care along the side of the road – be aware of traffic and do hop up on the grass verge when required.

When you reach a layby on your right, you can if you wish follow the footpath down to the water's edge of the pool seen to the right of the road. The pools of water were made to aid the lead working process in the 1850s.

One of the man-made pools

> ⓘ *The Mendip Hills are scattered with round barrows (burial chambers) from ancient times, such as those near Priddy.*

Continue along the road and when you see the wooden footpath sign on your left cross the road and follow the footpath, to join a wide, gravel pathway.

5 There are many criss-crossing paths in **Stockhill Woods** but follow the path right at the fork in the path. Follow this gravel pathway straight ahead until you see a narrower footpath on your right with a rustic wooden bench. This is a great spot to sit with your flask and a snack to listen to the birdsong. Continue along this path until you reach a path on your right marked 'Spruce Trail shortcut'. Enter the forest following the purple arrow left at a bench. At a T-junction in the path, turn right where the path leads back to the car park.

– To shorten
At Waypoint 5 omit the loop into the woods and follow the road all the way back to the car park. Saves 1km (about 20min).

+ To lengthen
Stockhill Woods has many trails and footpaths to explore. There are picnic benches and pre-marked routes to follow.

Roman mining and Bronze Age places of rest

This area is one of the highest points on Mendip and this walk is like a stroll through a living museum; with its craters, pockmarks and pools, there are clues all around you harking back to the lead mining which took place here from Roman times and continued well into the late 19th century.

The highest section of your walk at the Priddy Nine Barrows and Ashen Hill Barrows takes you to Bronze Age burial chambers which at their time of creation would have been an impressive landmark on the Mendip plateau. Even today, they offer an aura of peace and tranquillity.

WALK 15
Chew Valley Lake and Knowle Hill

Time 1hr 30min
Distance 5km (3.1 miles)
Climb 70m

Start/finish	Chew Valley Lake, Wally Lane, Chew Magna
Locate	///chins.forehead.enormous
Cafes/pubs	Restaurant and takeaway by lake
Transport	Bus 99 operated by The Big Lemon (limited service)
Parking	Car park at northern end of lake (BS40 8SZ)
Toilets	Next to restaurant

A stroll beside the lake, through woodland and up the hill for refreshing views before finishing with a lakeside cuppa

This relaxing walk is a blend of country lanes, peaceful footpaths, woodland wandering and a little climb which rewards you with a glorious lake view. Since the opening of the Salt & Malt restaurant in 2015, visitors can enjoy good locally sourced food and refreshments while enjoying the lakeside view.

The lake is popular with fishing and sailing enthusiasts

SHORT WALKS CHEDDAR AND THE MENDIPS

1 Begin by following the blue footpath signs for 'Chew Valley Lake Recreational Trail', with the lake to your right, leading to a secondary car park.

Opened in April 1956, Chew Valley Lake has been designated a Site of Special Scientific Interest (SSSI) due to its importance to wildlife. The lake is used for fishing (with permit) and by the Chew Valley Sailing Club for dinghy sailing.

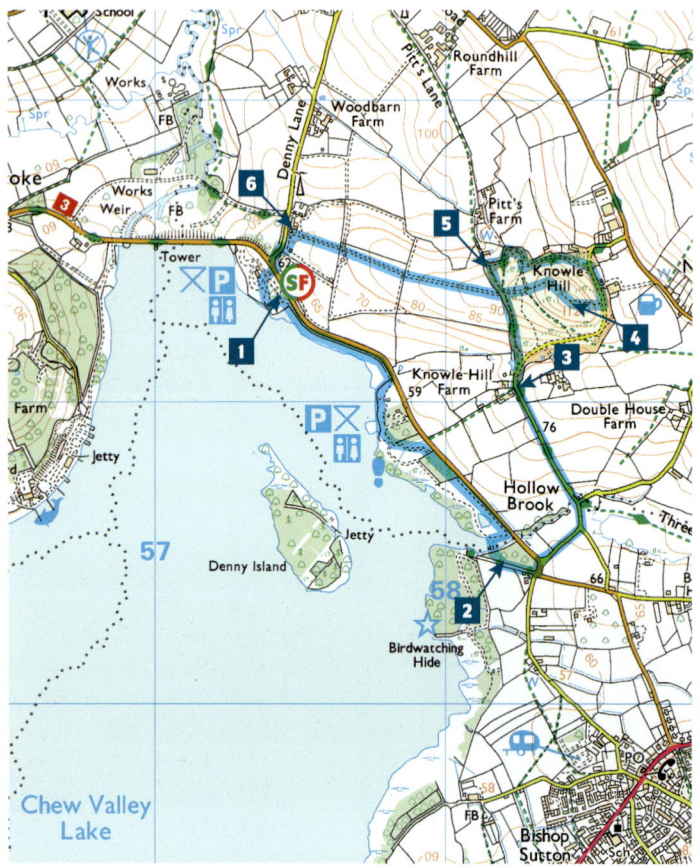

WALK 15 – CHEW VALLEY LAKE AND KNOWLE HILL

The walk alongside the lake makes for easy strolling

> ⓘ *Chew Valley Lake is the largest artificial freshwater lake in the South West and provides the city of Bristol with much of its drinking water.*

As the trail splits, take the left option (not the right for Grebe Trail). Follow the paved pathway, then cross the wooden bridge on your left, taking the path to your left. Pass through gates onto a lane and turn left.

2 You are now approaching a bit of a complicated junction. Bear left initially and then walk down the lane marked with a national speed limit sign. (Take care and walk on the grass verge to cross the junction.) When you reach a T-junction turn left, walking towards a stone cottage called Hollowbrook Cottage. Keep the cottage to your right and follow the lane straight ahead to pass Knowle House on your left.

SHORT WALKS CHEDDAR AND THE MENDIPS

Chew Valley Lake provides the ideal habitat for many birds

WALK 15 – CHEW VALLEY LAKE AND KNOWLE HILL

3 Continue along the lane for another 50m or so until you see a sign for a public footpath. Follow this sign left through the bracken and copse. As the path opens out into fern and heathland, you reach a crossroads. Turn right and walk up to the top of **Knowle Hill**. Take a seat on the bench and enjoy the view across the lake with the Mendip Hills in the far distance.

4 To descend, keep the bench to your left and the lake to your right and follow the path downhill towards farm buildings. Turn left as you join the lane passing a house called Orchardleigh on your right. Take the lane on your left marked with a footpath sign and T-junction sign for 'Private drive'. The lane loops around. Do not divert until you see a red-brick house a little way ahead (marked 'Private') and a footpath sign on your left which leads uphill with a wooden fence on your right. Continue uphill, passing Far End Cottage on your right.

5 With Knowle Hill away to your left, weave through the ferns. At a crossroads in the path, turn right and walk ahead through a gap in the hedgerow (to the left of a tree). **Chew Valley Lake** is now straight ahead. Follow this path across the field keeping the lake on your left. Continue into the next field along the gravel track, passing through an avenue of fruit trees towards farm buildings.

> ⓘ *The Mendip Hills are home to Somerset's county flower, the Cheddar Pink.*

The view from Knowle Hill

SHORT WALKS CHEDDAR AND THE MENDIPS

Walk through a gap in the hedge to see the lake ahead of you

6 Pass the farm buildings on your right. The driveway leads left before joining the road. Turn left, walk down the hill and join the grass verge on the left. Cross the road safely and walk back into the car park. The Salt & Malt is the perfect spot for post-walk refreshments, whether you opt for takeaway to sit lakeside, or prefer to enjoy the views from the restaurant.

— To shorten

If you don't fancy the short climb to Knowle Hill, turn left at the crossroads on the heathland after Waypoint 3, passing through a gap in the hedge to continue the route from Waypoint 5.

USEFUL INFORMATION

Tourism bodies

Mendip Hills National Landscape
www.mendiphills-nl.org.uk

Tourist information

Wells Tourist Information Centre
www.wellssomerset.com

Cheddar Visitor Information Centre
www.discovercheddar.co.uk

Travel

There are limited bus services within the Mendip Hills and services are subject to timetable and route changes.

For a comprehensive list of up-to-date services across Somerset see
www.bustimes.org

The Big Lemon (trialling routes via Chew Valley Lake)
www.thebiglemon.com

First Bus www.firstbus.co.uk

Even your four-legged friend will appreciate the reservoir views (Walk 7)

© Rachel Mead 2026
First edition 2026
ISBN: 978 1 78631 254 9
eISBN: 978 1 78765 230 9

Printed in Singapore by KHL Printing using responsibly sourced paper.
A catalogue record for this book is available from the British Library.
All photographs are by the author unless otherwise stated.

© Crown copyright and database rights 2026 OS AC0000810376

Cicerone's EU representative for GPSR compliance is Easy Access System Europe, Mustamäe tee 50, 10621 Tallinn, Estonia. Email gpsr.requests@easproject.com.

CICERONE

Cicerone Press, Juniper House, Murley Moss, Oxenholme Road,
Kendal, Cumbria, LA9 7RL

www.cicerone.co.uk

Updates to this Guide

While every effort is made to ensure the accuracy of guidebooks as they go to print, changes can occur during the lifetime of an edition. Any updates that we know of for this guide will be on the Cicerone website (www.cicerone.co.uk/1254/updates), so please check before planning your trip. We also advise that you check information about transport, accommodation and shops locally. Even rights of way can be altered over time. We are always grateful for information about any discrepancies between a guidebook and the facts on the ground, sent by email to updates@cicerone.co.uk.

Register your book: To sign up to receive free updates, special offers and GPX files where available, create a Cicerone account and register your purchase via the 'My Account' tab at www.cicerone.co.uk.